Forever Grateful To You:

Made in the USA
Coppell, TX
28 April 2022

77159788R00066